INTRODUC

"The Little Book of Golf Excuses" is a guide that delves into the world of genuine golf excuses that every golfer needs to remember!

This book takes a light-hearted approach to the common and not-so-common reasons for hitting bad shots on the golf course. Packed with over 101 reasons this pocket guide offers an extensive collection of excuses that golfers can use to absolve themselves of any responsibility for their errant shots.

This pocket guide explores the wide spectrum of excuses that golfers have at their disposal.

"The Little Book of Golf Excuses" emphasizes the universal experience of golfers seeking refuge from the frustration and challenges of the game by placing the blame on anything other than themselves.

This pocket guide is sure to resonate with golfers of all levels. Whether you're a beginner or a seasoned pro, "The Little Book of Golf Excuses" will remind you that golf is a game meant to be enjoyed, even when the shots don't go as planned.

So, grab your clubs, don your best poker face, and prepare to dive into the world of creative excuses as you make your way through the ups and downs of the golf course.

Could you spare a moment to make a world of difference in my journey?

Your review means the world to an Independent Author like me.

Please take a moment to leave a review and share your thoughts.

It really is appreciated.

THANK YOU!

SCAN ME

EXCUSE DELIVERY

Now before you arm yourself with an arsenal of creative golf excuses, it's important you take your excuse game to the next level. In this section, we present you with a collection of tips for delivering golf excuses with a straight face and a twinkle in the eye. After all, mastering the art of excuse delivery is essential to maximize the comedic impact and keep the fun going on the golf course.

Here are some tips for delivering golf excuses with a straight face and a twinkle in the eye, along with some examples:

- **Maintain a Deadpan Expression:** Keep a straight face while delivering your excuse, as if it's the most serious and plausible explanation in the world. The contrast between the seriousness of your expression and the absurdity of the excuse will amplify the comedic effect.

- **Use Dramatic Pause:** Pause for a moment before revealing your excuse, building anticipation and adding a touch of theatricality. This pause allows the tension to build and sets the stage for the punchline.

Example: "You see, I was aiming for that majestic oak tree on the left, but right at the last moment, it whispered to me, 'Choose the sand trap instead.' And well, I couldn't ignore the tree's advice, could I?"

- **Emphasize with Hand Gestures:** Use subtle hand gestures to add emphasis and flair to your excuse. Playfully point in different directions or mimic the motion of an object or creature to reinforce the absurdity of the situation.

Example: "As I swung, I felt a sudden disturbance in the force, like a wayward squirrel surfing on my club face. It had impeccable balance, I must say!"

"I know I am getting better at golf because I am hitting fewer spectators." - Gerald R. Ford

Maintain a Twinkle in the Eye: While keeping a straight face, let your eyes twinkle with mischief and humor. This subtle twinkle communicates to your fellow golfers that you're in on the joke and adds an extra layer of lightheartedness to the moment.

Example: "Oh, that bunker over there? Well, you see, it's not just sand. It's a secret teleportation device that randomly sends golf balls on unexpected adventures. I was just exploring its fascinating capabilities!"

Play with Sarcasm: Employ sarcasm to deliver your excuse in a tongue-in-cheek manner. Infuse your tone with a hint of irony to let your playing partners know that you're fully aware of the absurdity of your explanation.

Example: "Oh, yes, I intentionally aimed for the water hazard. You know, it's my secret strategy to check on the wildlife and keep the ecosystem in balance. I'm an environmentalist golfer, you see!"

Remember, the key to delivering excuses with a straight face and a twinkle in the eye is to strike a balance between conviction and playfulness. Practice these tips, adapt them to your personal style, and enjoy the laughter and camaraderie they bring to your golfing adventures!

"They say golf is like life, but don't believe them. Golf is more complicated than that." - Gardner Dickinson

Poor alignment: Incorrectly lining up your body and club face in relation to the target can result in wayward shots.

Grip issues: Holding the club too tightly or incorrectly can lead to inconsistent swings and mishits.

Lack of balance: Failing to maintain proper balance throughout the swing can cause misfires and loss of power.

Improper weight transfer: Not shifting your weight correctly from backswing to downswing can result in off-center hits.

Swing plane problems: Deviating from the correct swing path can cause slices, hooks, and other errant shots.

Incorrect ball position: Placing the ball too far forward or back in your stance can affect the club's impact with the ball.

Tension and stress: Feeling nervous or tense during your swing can lead to muscle tightness and loss of fluidity.

Lack of clubhead speed: Insufficient clubhead speed may result in shorter distances and difficulty getting the ball airborne.

Misjudging distances: Incorrectly gauging the yardage or wind conditions can lead to shots falling short or going long.

Fat or thin shots: Hitting the ground before the ball (fat shots) or striking the top half of the ball (thin shots) can cause inconsistent contact.

Lack of practice and technique: Insufficient practice and inadequate knowledge of proper golf techniques can lead to inconsistent shots.

"If you think it's hard to meet new people, try picking up the wrong golf ball." - Jack Lemmon

Mental distractions: Allowing external factors like noise, crowd, or personal thoughts to disrupt your focus can impact your swing.

Club selection: Choosing the wrong club for the shot at hand, whether due to misjudgment or lack of familiarity, can lead to poor results.

Course conditions: Challenging factors like heavy rough, strong winds, or uneven lies can make it harder to execute shots effectively.

Physical limitations: Certain physical restrictions, such as lack of flexibility or strength, can affect the quality of your swing.

Lack of focus: Allowing your mind to wander or losing concentration during your swing can lead to poor shot execution.

Poor course management: Making incorrect decisions regarding shot selection, aiming points, or risk assessment can result in unfavorable outcomes.

Timing and rhythm issues: Failing to synchronize the various components of your swing, such as the takeaway, transition, and impact, can result in inconsistent shots.

External distractions: Noise, movement, or other disturbances in the environment can disrupt your concentration and impact your shot quality.

Equipment issues: Using clubs that are ill-fitted for your swing, damaged, or in need of maintenance can affect your shots.

"The only thing a golfer needs is more daylight." - Ben Hogan

Weather conditions: Factors like rain, wind, or extreme temperatures can influence the flight of the ball and make it more challenging to achieve desired results.

Inadequate warm-up: Not properly warming up your muscles before a round of golf can lead to stiffness, restricted range of motion, and compromised swings.

Overthinking: Analyzing your swing mechanics excessively or trying to make too many adjustments during a round can hinder natural flow and cause poor shots.

Rushed or hurried swings: Feeling rushed or pressured to hit quickly can result in rushed swings, leading to loss of control and accuracy.

Lack of confidence: Doubting your abilities or feeling insecure about your shots can negatively impact your swing and overall performance.

Inconsistent pre-shot routine: Failing to establish a consistent and effective pre-shot routine can lead to inconsistency in swing execution.

Lack of adaptability: Failing to adjust your technique or shot strategy based on changing conditions or obstacles on the course can result in poor shots.

Shot selection errors: Choosing a shot type or strategy that is not suitable for the situation or your skill level can lead to unfavorable outcomes.

Unfavorable lies: Having the ball positioned in a difficult or awkward location, such as a divot, bunker, or rough, can make it challenging to execute a good shot.

"Golf is a puzzle without an answer. I've played the game for 50 years, and I still haven't the slightest idea of how to play." - Gary Player

Mental pressure: Feeling nervous, anxious, or experiencing performance anxiety can affect your ability to execute shots effectively.

Poor course knowledge: Insufficient understanding of the course layout, hazards, or optimal positioning can lead to strategic errors and bad shots.

Lack of visualization: Failing to mentally visualize and imagine the desired shot trajectory and landing spot can impact your execution.

Poor shot selection based on skill level: Attempting shots or techniques that are beyond your current skill level can result in inconsistent or inaccurate shots.

Lack of practice variety: Limited practice routines or failing to incorporate a variety of shots and scenarios can lead to difficulty adapting on the course.

Lack of flexibility: Insufficient flexibility in your muscles and joints can restrict your range of motion and impact the fluidity of your swing.

Inadequate clubface control: Failing to properly square the clubface at impact can result in shots that veer off-target.

Over-aggressiveness: Trying to hit every shot with maximum power and aggression can lead to loss of control and wayward shots.

Inconsistent tempo: Having an inconsistent rhythm or pace in your swing can make it difficult to achieve consistent contact and ball flight.

Poor ball contact: Hitting the ball too high or low on the clubface, can result in poor distance and accuracy.

"Golfer: 'My golf is awful, I think I'm going to drown myself in the lake.' Caddy: 'Think you can keep your head down for that long?'"

Lack of self-awareness: Failing to recognize and address recurring swing flaws or tendencies can lead to repeated mistakes and bad shots.

Mental interference from previous shots: Lingering frustration or dwelling on previous bad shots can impact your focus and execution on subsequent shots.

Lack of course strategy: Neglecting to develop a game plan for navigating the course and strategically selecting shots can lead to poor decision-making.

Lack of confidence in specific shots: Having doubts or lack of confidence in executing certain shots, such as bunker shots or long putts, can affect your performance.

Incorrect club selection: Choosing a club that doesn't match the required distance or shot trajectory can lead to suboptimal results.

Lack of adaptability to course conditions: Failing to adjust your approach based on factors like the firmness of the fairways, speed of the greens, or changing weather conditions can affect your shots.

Poor course management: Making strategic errors like taking unnecessary risks or failing to account for course hazards can lead to unfavorable outcomes.

Distractions from fellow players: Noise, movement, or conversations from other players in your group can disrupt your focus and impact your shots.

Physical discomfort or pain: Dealing with physical ailments like back pain, joint stiffness, or fatigue can affect your ability to swing freely and consistently.

Golf is a game where you yell "Fore", shoot six and write down five –
Napolean Hill

Misalignment of body and target: Not properly aligning your body, feet, hips, and shoulders with the intended target can cause shots to veer off-course.

Lack of practice on specific shots: Neglecting to practice shots that are frequently encountered on the course, such as chip shots or awkward lies, can lead to inconsistency in execution.

Over-reliance on mechanical thoughts: Becoming too consumed with swing mechanics and technical thoughts during the swing can hinder your natural fluidity and timing.

Poor course visualization: Failing to mentally visualize the desired shot path and landing area before executing the shot can lead to misjudgment and poor execution.

Lack of patience and composure: Allowing frustration or impatience to affect your mindset and decision-making can result in rushed and poorly executed shots.

Grip pressure inconsistency: Inconsistency in grip pressure throughout the swing can lead to inconsistent clubface control and shot outcomes.

Lack of focus on the target: Focusing too much on swing mechanics or internal thoughts instead of the target can result in misalignment and off-target shots.

Poor course reconnaissance: Failing to study and understand the layout of the course, including yardages, hazards, and green undulations, can lead to misjudgments and poor shot selection.

Lack of confidence in certain shots: Having doubts or fear when faced with challenging shots, such as long carries over water or tight fairways, can affect your swing and result in subpar shots.

There are three roads to ruin; women, gambling, and golf. The most pleasant is with women, the quickest is with gambling, but the surest is with golf. – Andrew Perry

Neglecting to adjust for elevation changes: Not considering the effect of uphill or downhill slopes on club selection and shot trajectory can lead to misjudged distances and inconsistent results.

Lack of mental resilience: Allowing previous bad shots or a string of poor holes to negatively impact your mental state can result in a loss of focus and confidence, leading to more bad shots.

Poor timing in the swing: Failing to synchronize the movement of your body, arms, and hands can lead to mistimed swings and inconsistent contact with the ball.

Lack of awareness of swing tendencies: Not recognizing recurring swing flaws or tendencies, such as a tendency to pull or slice the ball, can lead to repeated mistakes and inconsistent shots.

Improper ball position in relation to the stance: Placing the ball too far forward or back in your stance can affect the angle of attack and impact the desired ball flight.

Lack of mental commitment to the shot: Failing to fully commit mentally to the shot, whether due to doubt, distraction, or indecision, can lead to tentative swings and poor execution.

Misreading green breaks and speeds: Misjudging the slope and speed of the greens can result in misread putts and inconsistent distance control on longer putts.

Poor posture and setup: Incorrect posture and setup position can affect your balance, stability, and swing mechanics, leading to inconsistent shots.

Golfer: 'Do you think I can get there with a 5-iron?'

Caddy: 'Eventually'

Excessive tension in the hands and arms: Gripping the club too tightly or having excessive tension in the hands and arms can restrict the natural flow of the swing and result in poor shots.

Lack of proper weight shift: Failing to transfer your weight properly from backswing to downswing can lead to loss of power, inconsistency, and loss of control.

Not adjusting for wind: Neglecting to account for wind direction and strength can result in misjudged shots and unpredictable ball flight.

Inadequate visual focus: Failing to maintain a clear focus on the ball throughout the swing can affect your timing, club face control, and overall shot quality.

Poor ball flight control: Inability to control the desired shot shape, such as fading or drawing the ball, can lead to inconsistent ball flights and difficulty navigating the course.

Ignoring physical limitations: Not recognizing and adapting to your physical limitations, such as flexibility, strength, or range of motion, can hinder your ability to execute certain shots effectively.

Lack of mental focus during practice: Going through the motions during practice sessions without maintaining focused attention on each shot can hinder skill development and lead to inconsistency on the course.

Poor course conditions: Playing on courses with poorly maintained fairways, inconsistent greens, or untrimmed rough can make it challenging to execute clean shots.

Golf is an easy game...

It's just hard to play.

Overconfidence: Being overly confident and underestimating the difficulty of a shot or the course can lead to complacency and careless mistakes.

Lack of adaptability to different grass types: Inability to adjust your swing and shot technique based on the type of grass you are playing on (e.g., Bermuda grass, bentgrass) can affect your contact and control.

Lack of feedback and analysis: Not utilizing video analysis, swing feedback, or professional instruction to identify and address swing flaws can hinder improvement and lead to persistent bad shots.

Poor course knowledge regarding green speed: Failing to consider the speed of the greens when putting can lead to misjudged putts, both in terms of line and pace.

Inconsistent pre-shot routine: Having a disorganized or rushed pre-shot routine can affect your mental preparation, focus, and ability to execute shots consistently.

Lack of visualization on approach shots: Not visualizing the intended landing area, shot trajectory, and spin on approach shots can lead to poor distance control and missed greens.

Over-reliance on technology: Relying too heavily on swing analysis apps, launch monitors, or distance-measuring devices during practice and play can distract from the feel and artistry of the game.

Poor recovery shot execution: Failing to assess and strategize effectively when faced with challenging situations, such as being in the trees or deep rough, can result in unsuccessful recovery shots.

If you get caught on the course during a storm and are afraid of lightning, then hold up your one-iron; even god cannot hit a one-iron. – Lee Trevino

Neglecting to practice short game shots: Insufficient practice on chipping, pitching, and bunker shots can lead to inconsistency around the greens and wasted strokes.

Lack of awareness of body position at impact: Failing to maintain proper posture and position at impact, such as a stable lower body and square shoulders, can lead to inconsistent contact and off-target shots.

Overcompensation for previous mistakes: Trying too hard to correct a specific swing flaw or compensate for previous bad shots can result in overcorrection and new swing issues.

Poor shot visualization and target selection: Failing to visualize the shot path, select a specific target, and commit to it can lead to indecision, mishits, and missed opportunities.

Lack of mental preparation for pressure situations: Not mentally rehearsing and preparing for high-pressure shots, such as crucial putts or tee shots on difficult holes, can lead to tension and poor performance.

Inadequate rest and recovery: Playing golf without sufficient rest and recovery between rounds or practice sessions can lead to physical and mental fatigue, affecting performance.

Excessive focus on outcome rather than process: Being too fixated on the result of the shot instead of focusing on proper technique and execution can lead to unnecessary pressure and tension.

Neglecting to analyze and learn from mistakes: Failing to reflect on and learn from previous rounds, shot patterns, and mistakes can hinder progress and result in repeating the same errors.

Why am I using a new putter?
Because the old one didn't float too well. —
Craig Stadler

Ineffective use of practice aids: Using training aids incorrectly or relying too heavily on them without understanding their purpose and limitations can lead to dependency and ineffective practice.

Lack of trust in your swing: Doubting your swing mechanics or second-guessing your technique during the swing can lead to tension and a breakdown in the fluidity of your motion.

Over-analysis of swing mechanics: Obsessively dissecting every aspect of your swing mechanics without allowing natural athleticism and feel to come into play can hinder your performance and inhibit your ability to hit good shots.

Misjudgment of yardages: Incorrectly estimating distances to the target or failing to account for factors such as elevation changes, wind, or temperature can result in club selection errors and missed greens.

Lack of enjoyment and fun: Forgetting to have fun and enjoy the game can create unnecessary pressure and tension, leading to inhibited performance and an increased likelihood of hitting bad shots.

Poor ball selection: Not selecting the right ball for your swing speed, spin preferences, and playing conditions can affect your control, feel, and overall shot performance.

Lack of adaptability to different golf formats: Not adjusting your strategy, shot selection, and mindset when playing different formats of golf, such as stroke play, match play, or scramble, can impact your results.

Lack of commitment to ongoing improvement: Failing to invest time, effort, and resources in continuous learning, skill development, and seeking guidance can limit your progress and potential in the game.

"Golf is a game that's not so much about the ball going where you want it to as it is about not going where you don't want it to." - Unknown

Fatigue: Physical or mental fatigue can affect your coordination, leading to less precise swings and diminished performance.

Poor club fitting: Using clubs that are not properly fitted to your swing characteristics, such as incorrect shaft flex, length, or clubhead design, can lead to inconsistent results.

Difficulty managing nerves and adrenaline: Struggling to control nerves and the adrenaline rush in high-pressure situations, such as in competitions or important rounds, can lead to heightened tension and erratic shots.

Lack of adaptability to different pin positions: Failing to adjust your approach and club selection based on pin position, such as front, middle, or back of the green, can result in missed opportunities and challenging birdie putts.

Inadequate hydration and nutrition: Not properly hydrating or fueling your body during the round can lead to physical fatigue, decreased focus, and diminished performance.

Inability to control adrenaline on tee shots: Experiencing a surge of adrenaline on tee shots, leading to a rushed swing and decreased accuracy.

Inability to handle playing partners' performance: Allowing the performance of playing partners, whether exceptionally good or poor, to distract or affect your own game.

Loss of focus on the back nine: Experiencing mental fatigue or a decrease in concentration on the second half of the round can lead to mistakes and higher scores.

"I'm hitting the woods just great, but I'm having a terrible time getting out of them." - Harry Tofcano

Ineffective use of course management tools: Not utilizing tools such as yardage books, course maps, or GPS devices to properly strategize and navigate the course can result in poor decision-making.

Lack of practice with different ball positions: Insufficient practice hitting shots from various ball positions, such as uphill, downhill, or sidehill lies, can lead to difficulty adapting during the round.

Over reliance on a single shot shape: Relying too heavily on a particular shot shape, such as always playing a fade or draw, can limit your shot options and versatility.

Inability to maintain a consistent swing tempo throughout the round: Allowing the swing tempo to fluctuate during the course of a round can lead to inconsistency in timing and contact.

Difficulty controlling trajectory: Struggling to control the trajectory of your shots, such as hitting the ball too high or too low, can limit your ability to navigate challenging course conditions.

Inconsistent strike location on the club face: Failing to consistently strike the ball in the center of the club face can lead to loss of distance, accuracy, and control.

Ineffective club grip: Holding the club with improper grip pressure or incorrect hand placement can affect swing mechanics and lead to errant shots.

Over reliance on technique over feel: Being too focused on technical swing mechanics rather than relying on feel and natural instincts can lead to robotic swings and decreased shot creativity.

"I'm not saying my golf game went bad, but if I grew tomatoes, they'd come up sliced." - Lee Trevino

Facts and Stats About Golf -
That will help excuse your bad play!

According to England Golf, the average handicap for male golfers is 17.2, while the average handicap for female golfers is 27.2 This is based on data from over 400,000 golfers who have submitted scores through the My England Golf app.

The average handicap for male golfers in the United States is 18.6. The average handicap for female golfers in the United States is 26.6.

According to the National Golf Foundation, the average score for an 18-hole round of golf is around 90 strokes for recreational male golfers and approximately 105 strokes for recreational female golfers.

According to the National Golf Foundation, approximately 55% of golfers break a score of 100 on an 18-hole course regularly. This means that more than half of the golfers who play the sport achieve scores of 100 or lower. That means approximately 45% do not!

According to the United States Golf Association (USGA), approximately 1.85% of male golfers and 0.69% of female golfers have a single-figure handicap. This means that they are among the top 2% of golfers in the United States.

To put this into perspective, there are approximately 24.2 million golfers in the United States. This means that there are approximately 44,200 male golfers and 18,500 female golfers with a single-figure handicap.
scores in this range.

Golfer: 'You've got to be the worst caddy in the world'

Caddy: 'Surely not!, that would be too much of a coincidence'

The average scores of 9 handicap golfers and scratch golfers - Male

9 Handicap Golfer	Scratch Golfer
Average Score	
84	70
Average Drive Distance	
233 yards	259 yards
Average Fairway Hit %	
46%	51%
Average Green in Regulation %	
28%	56%
Average Putts per Round	
32.2	30.7
Average Strokes Gained Off the Tee	
-1.0	1.1
Average Strokes Gained Approach	
-0.5	1.3
Average Strokes Gained Putting	
-0.7	1.0

The average scores of 18 handicap golfers and scratch golfers - Male

18 Handicap Golfer	Scratch Golfer
Average Score	
90	70
Average Drive Distance	
217 yards	259 yards
Average Fairway Hit %	
42%	51%
Average Green in Regulation %	
23%	56%
Average Putts per Round	
36.2	30.7
Average Strokes Gained Off the Tee	
-1.8	1.1
Average Strokes Gained Approach	
-0.8	1.3
Average Strokes Gained Putting	
-1.2	1.0

The average scores of 24 handicap golfers and scratch golfers - Male

24 Handicap Golfer   **Scratch Golfer**

Average Score
102   70

Average Drive Distance
197 yards   259 yards

Average Fairway Hit %
32%   51%

Average Green in Regulation %
13%   56%

Average Putts per Round
44.2   30.7

Average Strokes Gained Off the Tee
-3.8   1.1

Average Strokes Gained Approach
-1.8   1.3

Average Strokes Gained Putting
2.2   1.0

The average scores of 30 handicap golfers and scratch golfers - Male

30 Handicap Golfer	Scratch Golfer
Average Score	
108	70
Average Drive Distance	
187 yards	259 yards
Average Fairway Hit %	
27%	51%
Average Green in Regulation %	
8%	56%
Average Putts per Round	
48.2	30.7
Average Strokes Gained Off the Tee	
-4.8	1.1
Average Strokes Gained Approach	
-2.3	1.3
Average Strokes Gained Putting	
-2.7	1.0

The average scores of 9 handicap golfers and scratch golfers - Female

9 Handicap Golfer   **Scratch Golfer**

Average Score

83   74

Average Drive Distance

167 yards   210 yards

Average Fairway Hit %

27%   42%

Average Green in Regulation %

18%   45%

Average Putts per Round

48.2   33.7

Average Strokes Gained Off the Tee

-4.8   0.3

Average Strokes Gained Approach

-2.3   0.8

Average Strokes Gained Putting

-2.7   0.5

The average scores of 18 handicap golfers and scratch golfers - Female

18 Handicap Golfer	Scratch Golfer
Average Score	
90	74
Average Drive Distance	
157 yards	210 yards
Average Fairway Hit %	
22%	42%
Average Green in Regulation %	
13%	45%
Average Putts per Round	
52.2	33.7
Average Strokes Gained Off the Tee	
-6.8	0.3
Average Strokes Gained Approach	
-3.3	0.8
Average Strokes Gained Putting	
-3.7	0.5

The average scores of 24 handicap golfers and scratch golfers - Female

24 Handicap Golfer	Scratch Golfer
Average Score	
96	74
Average Drive Distance	
157 yards	210 yards
Average Fairway Hit %	
22%	42%
Average Green in Regulation %	
13%	45%
Average Putts per Round	
52.2	33.7
Average Strokes Gained Off the Tee	
-6.8	0.3
Average Strokes Gained Approach	
-3.3	0.8
Average Strokes Gained Putting	
-3.7	0.5

The average scores of 30 handicap golfers and scratch golfers - Female

30 Handicap Golfer	Scratch Golfer
Average Score	
112	74
Average Drive Distance	
167 yards	210 yards
Average Fairway Hit %	
22%	42%
Average Green in Regulation %	
5%	45%
Average Putts per Round	
52.2	33.7
Average Strokes Gained Off the Tee	
-5.8	0.3
Average Strokes Gained Approach	
-3.3	0.8
Average Strokes Gained Putting	
-3.7	0.5

As we come to the end of "The Little Book of Golf Excuses," we'd like to extend our sincerest thanks to you, dear reader. We hope that this journey through the realm of golf excuses has brought a smile to your face, lightened your golfing woes, and reminded you of the joy that comes with playing this wonderful game.

We understand that golf can be frustrating at times. It tests our patience, challenges our skills, and humbles us when we least expect it. But amidst the missed shots, lost balls, and wayward putts, there's something truly magical about the game. It brings us together, creates lasting memories, and provides us with endless opportunities to connect with fellow golf enthusiasts.

"The Little Book of Golf Excuses" is our way of celebrating the lighter side of golf. It's a tribute to the camaraderie, laughter, and shared experiences that make this sport so special. We hope that the excuses have entertained and inspired you to approach the game with a lighthearted perspective.

In closing, we want to express our heartfelt appreciation for joining us on this journey. Thank you for allowing us to be a part of your golfing adventures, both on and off the course. We hope that whenever you find yourself facing a challenging shot or an unexpected outcome, you'll remember the power of a well-placed excuse and a good laugh.

May your future rounds be filled with memorable shots, remarkable recoveries, and, of course, an abundance of laughter. And remember, dear reader, that no matter what happens on the golf course, the most important thing is to cherish the moments, embrace the imperfections, and enjoy the wonderful game of golf.

Could you spare a moment to make a world of difference in my journey?

Your review means the world to an Independent Author like me.

Please take a moment to leave a review and share your thoughts .

It really is appreciated.

THANK YOU!

Enjoyed this book?

How about some of the other titles in the series?

Share the gift of humor with someone you know, and make them smile!

Printed in Great Britain
by Amazon

35983506R00026